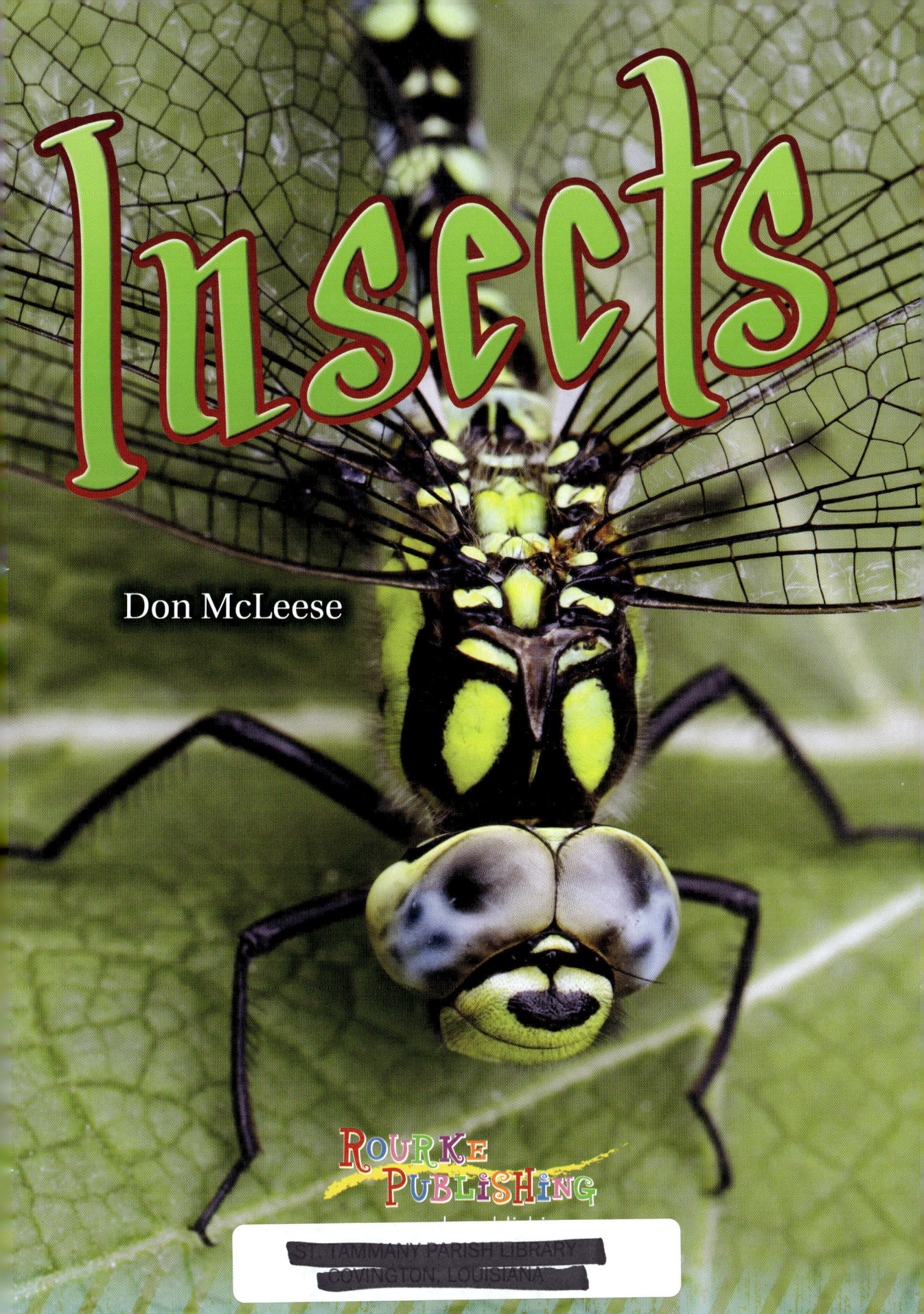

Insects

Don McLeese

Rourke Publishing

© 2012 Rourke Publishing LLC

All rights reserved. No part of this book may be reproduced or utilized in any form or by any means, electronic or mechanical including photocopying, recording, or by any information storage and retrieval system without permission in writing from the publisher.

www.rourkepublishing.com

PHOTO CREDITS: Cover © Sunheyy; Title Page © Cathy Keifer; Table of Contents © Lane V. Erickson; Page 4 © Vaclav Volrab, Insuratelu Gabriela Gianina; Page 5 © Mitya, Snookless; Page 6 © Dmitrijs Bindemanis, worldswildlifewonders; Page 7 © Morgan Lane Photography, stocksnapp; Page 8/9 © iliuta goean; Page 8 © manfredxy, vblinov; Page 9 © vblinov; Page 10/11 © Doug Lemke; Page 10 © Cathy Keifer, irishman; Page 11 © Goran Kapor; Page 12 © Dmitrijs Bindemanis, D. Kucharski & K. Kucharska, ex0rzist; Page 13 © Sherry Yates Sowell, David Parsons; Page 14/15 © Wallenrock; Page 15 © Alekcey; Page 16/17 © Kristina Postnikova; Page 17 © Cosmin Manci; Page 18 © Nick Barounis; Page 19 © Fotokostic; Page 20/21 © Smit; Page 22 © NitroCephal; Page Header © tonyz20

Edited by Precious McKenzie

Cover Design by Renee Brady
Layout by Nicola Stratford, Blue Door Publishing, FL

Library of Congress Cataloging-in-Publication Data

McLeese, Don
 Insects / Don McLeese
 p. cm. -- (Eye to Eye With Animals)
 ISBN 978-1-61741-778-8 (hard cover) (alk. paper)
 ISBN 978-1-61741-980-5 (soft cover)
 Library of Congress Control Number: 2011924824

Rourke Publishing
Printed in the United States of America, North Mankato, Minnesota
091610
091510LP-B

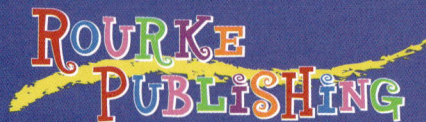

www.rourkepublishing.com - rourke@rourkepublishing.com
Post Office Box 643328 Vero Beach, Florida 32964

Table of Contents

What's Bugging You? 4
The Weird, Wonderful World of Insects . . 6
How Insects Grow 8
Are Insects Good or Bad For Us? 12
What Should We Do About Insects? . . . 18
Glossary 23
Index 24
Websites to Visit/About the Author 24

Chapter 1

What's Bugging You?

We live in a world of insects. Of the one and a half million kinds of animals identified by scientists, about a million are insects. Insects live almost everywhere, except deep in the ocean. Many swarm in the hottest jungles, but others live in the coldest areas, like the North Pole.

Scientists discover as many as 10,000 new kinds of insects every year. They think there may be many millions that have yet to be discovered.

Bumble Bee

June Beetle

Green Damselfly

Insects have six legs and they have no backbone. Creatures, like insects, without backbones are called **invertebrates**. Some insects such as butterflies have wings, while others such as ants do not have wings. Insects are sometimes known as bugs, but not all bugs are insects. The spider, for example, isn't an insect. This is because spiders have eight legs, not six.

Wolf Spider

Many people think spiders are insects but they aren't. They are arachnids.

Chapter 2
The Weird, Wonderful World of Insects

Without noses, insects smell with their **antennae**. Some of them taste with their feet and hear with the hairs on their bodies!

Insects have no lungs, but breathe through very small holes called spiracles on the sides of their bodies.

Interesting Insect Facts

Mosquito

The wings of a mosquito beat 500 times a second!

Ant

An ant can lift 50 times as much weight as its own body. Can you lift 50 times your body weight?

In addition to having six legs, all insects have three parts to their bodies. These parts are the head, the **thorax**, and the **abdomen**. The head is at the front of the insect. The head has eyes, a mouth, and antennae, or feelers. They use these antennae for touching and smelling. The thorax is the middle of the body. This is usually where the legs grow.

antennae

head

thorax

abdomen

Some insects have ears in their thorax as well. The last and largest section of the insect is the abdomen. This is where the insect breathes through spiracles.

You also have an abdomen- that is where your stomach is!

Chapter 3

How Insects Grow

Insects grow through stages. They start as eggs. Then they go through **metamorphosis**, a word that means change. Because there are so many kinds of insects, there are different kinds of metamorphosis. A simple insect will go through three stages of incomplete metamorphosis, changing from an egg into a **nymph**, a smaller version of the adult insect that sheds its skin several times as it gets bigger. Then it becomes an adult.

Shedding your skin is hard work! This dragonfly nymph will shed its skin several times before it becomes an adult dragonfly.

A butterfly is one type of insect that experiences a complete metamorphosis. It changes into **larva** instead of a nymph. During the larva stage as a caterpillar, it looks nothing like a butterfly. Then comes the **pupa** stage, or **chrysalis**. When it breaks out of the chrysalis, the insect has grown wings and becomes a brightly colored butterfly!

A caterpillar changing into a pupa.

A fully formed pupa is a chrysalis.

With the change complete, a butterfly emerges from its chrysalis.

Chapter 4
Are Insects Good or Bad for Us?

Insects bother most people, although many people seem to love butterflies! But, less than one percent of insects are harmful to humans. Insects that bite, like mosquitoes, can annoy people and a few insects have deadly poisons.

BITING & STINGING INSECTS

Mosquitoes

Wasps

Mosquitoes can transmit West Nile Encephalitis and malaria.

A wasp sting can kill a person if that person is allergic to wasps.

Boll Weevil

Some insects destroy crops. Boll weevils can destroy crops of cotton or corn.

Insects are crucial to the lives of plants because they pollinate them. Bees, moths, butterflies, and other flying insects carry **pollen** to plants that allows flowers to bloom and fruit to grow.

▲ The pollen sticks to the insect's body. When the insect lands on a new plant, the insect leaves the old pollen there, helping the new plant reproduce.

Praying mantis are insect predators. They use their front legs to capture other insects, like grasshoppers.

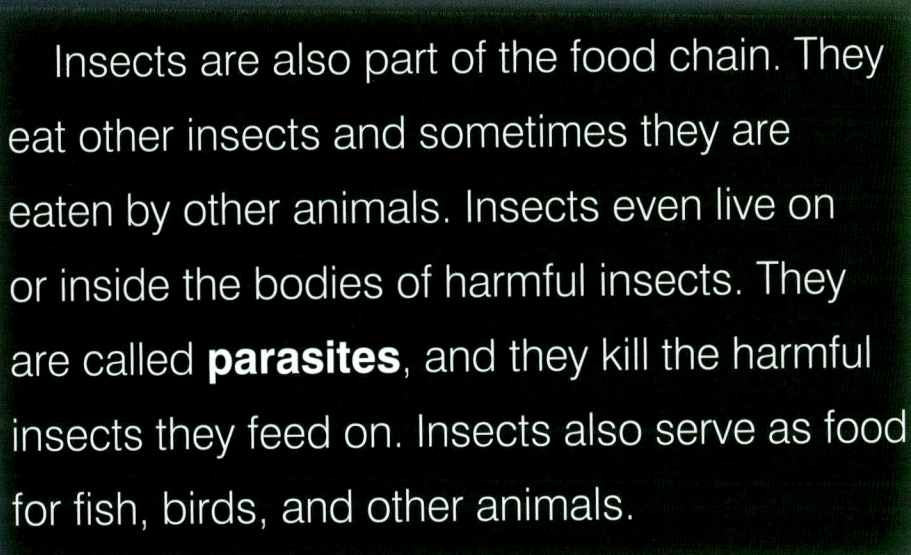

Insects are also part of the food chain. They eat other insects and sometimes they are eaten by other animals. Insects even live on or inside the bodies of harmful insects. They are called **parasites**, and they kill the harmful insects they feed on. Insects also serve as food for fish, birds, and other animals.

Although tiny, fleas have gained a bad reputation throughout history. They spread plague throughout Europe for hundreds of years.

Chapter 5
What Should We Do About Insects?

We often attempt to kill insects that bother us by poisoning the insects with insecticides. But such poisons can also get into our food and water supplies, hurting the environment.

There are other ways for people to keep insects away without using poison. One way to do this is to use citronella. Citronella is a plant that can be made into lotions or candles. Other plants that keep some insects away include rosemary and sage.

◂◂ *Rather than use harmful chemicals such as DEET, many people use citronella candles. Insects do not like the smell of citronella and will fly away from it.*

Researchers are experimenting with new chemicals that will control bothersome insect populations without harming people or the environment.

Although we can try to control the population of insects, in general, we have to learn to live with them. After all, there are a whole lot more of them than there are of us.

Many people turn to natural methods to prevent the infestation of insects into their homes. Some people like it when lizards, spiders, and birds live near their homes because those are nature's pest controllers!

Scientists believe that insects have been around longer than man has, perhaps since the prehistoric era. If all the other animals on Earth were to die somehow, insects could be the last survivors because there are just so many of them and they have proven to be adaptable over millions of years.

▼ Scientists discovered insects fossilized in amber, proving that insects were around during the time of dinosaurs!

Glossary

abdomen (AB-duh-muhn): the rear part of an insect's body

antennae (an-TEN-ee): the feelers on the head of an insect

chrysalis (KRISS-uh-liss): the stage of a butterfly's life between caterpillar and adulthood

invertebrates (in-VUR-tuh-brits): animals without backbones

larva (LAR-vuh): the worm-like stage of an insect's development after the egg

metamorphosis (met-uh-MOR-fuh-siss): a series of changes

nymph (NIMF): a young insect that sheds its skin

parasites (PAR-uh-sites): animals that live on or inside another animal and feed off of it

pollen (POL-uhn): tiny grains produced by flowering plants

pupa (PYOO-puh): the stage of an insect's development, when it is inactive, right before it becomes an adult

thorax (THOR-aks): the part of an insect's body between the head and the abdomen

Index

abdomen(s) 7
adult 8
antennae 6, 7
boll weevil 13
bugs 5
butterflies 5, 12, 14
caterpillar 10
chrysalis 10, 11
feelers 7
food chain 17
invertebrates 5
larva 10
metamorphosis 8, 10
nymph 8, 10
parasites 17
pollen 14, 15
pollinate 14
pupa 10
spiracles 6, 7
thorax 7

Websites To Visit

www.enchantedlearning.com/themes/insects.shtml www.insects.org

www.earthlife.net/insects/six.html

www.livescience.com/insects

www.insectimages.org

About the Author

Don McLeese is a journalism professor at the University of Iowa. He has written many articles for newspapers and magazines and many books for young students as well.